PUBLIC LIBRARY
Oskaloosa, Iowa

WITHDRAWN

Wilderness World

Survival

To Derek, Matt, and Zachary

May you be free and happy
in the wilderness world.

Survival

by Paul Neimark
illustrations by Tom Dunnington
Created by Zachary's Workshop LTD
Consulting Editor
Tom Opre
Midwest Field Editor
Field & Stream Magazine

CHILDRENS PRESS, CHICAGO

Picture Acknowledgement:
U.S.D.A.—UNITED STATES FOREST SERVICE—front cover, pages 1, 7, 9, 10, 12, 14, 23, 24, 28
WISCONSIN TRAVEL BUREAU—pages 8, 11, 13

Library of Congress Cataloging in Publication Data

Neimark, Paul G
 Survival.

 ((Wilderness world)
 SUMMARY: A guide for surviving in the wilderness, including signaling for help; locating drinking water and shelter; sleeping; using fire; keeping cool or warm; protecting against wind, rain, and animals; and treating inuries.
 1. Wilderness survival—Juvenile literature.
 [1. Wilderness survival. 2. Survival] I. Dunnington, Tom. II. Zachary's Workshop. III. Title. IV. Series.
 GV200.5.N43   613.6'9   80-39688
 ISBN 0-516-02454-X

Copyright© 1981 by Regensteiner Publishing Enterprises, Inc.
All rights reserved. Published simultaneously in Canada.
Printed in the United States of America.

 3 4 5 6 7 8 9 10 R 90 89 88 87 86 85 84 83

Contents

1... Lost! 7
2... Found! 13
3... Good Water—Bad Water 19
4... A New Home 25
5... Making a Fire—Escaping a Fire 31
6... Beating Heat and Cold 37
7... Beating the Weather 41
8... Avoiding Accidents 45
9... Attack! 49
10... Avoiding Infection 54
11... The Wilderness is Yours............ 57
For Further Reading 60
Index 61

Chapter 1

Lost!

What would you do if you were lost and alone on a snowy mountain?

That's what happened to twelve-year-old Jim.

His parents had taken him and his sister to Colorado for Christmas vacation. While his family was resting at the hotel, Jim went exploring on his own. He walked in what seemed a straight line from the lodge, making marks in the snow near trees and bushes so he'd have a trail to follow back. But soon it began snowing again. And Jim had become so interested in what was in front of him, that all of a sudden nothing was behind him!

He ran toward what looked like a familiar tree and brushed away the snow. There was no mark.

Opposite: The mountains never wait for Christmas. Their "snowcaps" stay on all year long—making trailmarking tricky. Pages 8-9: Jim should have realized that his tracks would be covered by windblown or new-fallen snow. Now he is lost!

He ran to a bush a short distance away. There was something that looked like his mark, but he couldn't be sure.

He raced to another tree, then another. Was that the mark he had made? It was so hard to tell. He could only guess which way to go.

Two hours later, Jim knew he had guessed wrong. He was lost on the side of a mountain. An ocean of snow was everywhere around him.

He huddled against a large tree to protect himself against the chilling wind. The sun was going down in the western sky. He remembered that the sun had been on the other side of the lodge when he first started out. But he had circled so much that he could be anywhere now. Maybe if he went toward the sun, he would find his way.

It was dark. Jim felt more alone than he ever had in his life.

He knew that his parents soon would be out looking for him. But he also knew that in the dark, with all this space for miles and miles, there was hardly any chance he would be found tonight. If only he could make it to the morning! But the wind was growing cold. He was hungry. He had no shelter, no weapons. And he was afraid.

Yet sometimes when you are the most afraid, you become the bravest. "I'm going to make it till morning—somehow," Jim said to himself.

Shortly after the sun rose the next day a search party found Jim — alive and well, though very cold and tired and hungry.

How did Jim do it? How should you do it? Soon you'll know the answers to those questions — and not only if you are lost on a deserted mountainside . . . but in the middle of a scorching desert . . . or in a forest facing an angry bear . . . or in the path of a cyclone . . . or in the heat and damp of a swamp.

You will learn how to write an S.O.S. in the snow or on the sand so that people in an airplane can see your signal.

You will learn how to take an old metal can, aim it at the sun, and signal far away.

You will learn how to escape wild animals, overcome heat, cold, raging winds, and exploding waters.

You will learn how to survive . . . if you keep your cool and know what to do.

As Jim did.

Chapter 2

Found!

Was Jim afraid? Sure he was. But he knew a couple of important things about fear, too.

First, he knew that all people are afraid—though some might not admit it—when they are lost. It's better to admit your fear, because then you can overcome it. The best way to overcome fear is to think about what you are going to do to protect yourself from wilderness enemies—and survive. That is what this book is all about. But remember: Fear can be your biggest enemy—only if you fear it.

Jim's parents were as happy as could be to have him back. But they were not happy that he had gone off alone. No one should ever go into the wilderness alone, especially without the proper equipment. Still, his mom and dad were glad he was smart

Opposite: "S.O.S." is an important code to remember. It is a call for help known all over the world. Pages 14-15: It is smart to check a place of shelter before using it. Snow can hide deep holes or unfriendly animals.

enough to find a safe shelter between two old logs for the night.

As soon as Jim knew he was lost, he began to signal so that someone could discover where he was. A good idea before you go anywhere near wilderness is to plan a simple signal. Agree that everyone will carry the signaling device—a whistle, white cloth, or flashlight will usually do—at all times.

One of the best ways to signal is to wave a piece of clothing from the end of a stick. When you signal, stand at the highest point you can easily find. Choose something that will stand out against the ground. In a green-and-brown wooded area, use something white. If you are on a desert or in snowy country, use a bright or dark color.

Sometimes you can "write" a call for help on the ground. In snow, form the letters "S.O.S." with branches and twigs. The larger the letters are, the better. On sand, stones and shrubs can make an S.O.S.

At night or on a cloudy day, a flashlight will attract attention. Fire attracts attention anytime. See Chapter 5 to learn how to build one safely. Hold a moist piece of clothing over the fire and then move it away to make smoke signals. Hold a mirror or a piece of metal—an old can will do—to the sun and flash "off" and "on." Anything that reflects light will make this kind of signal. A luminous strip from your clothing might even do the trick.

People, like animals, use all five senses—sight, touch, taste, hearing, smell—to track things down. Use all the different sense signals to catch rescuers' attention when you are lost.

Noise attracts attention, too. You can yell, whistle, or hit one shoe against the other.

One thing about being lost: You don't know how long you will be lost. So don't waste your energy, or anything else you have with you, from water to matches. Once someone does spot you, stay where you were when you were seen until your rescuer is right there with you.

Chapter 3

Good Water– Bad Water

When you are out in the wilderness, two things are most important. You must protect yourself against danger. You must also have good, clean water to drink.

Safe drinking water can be hard to find. You need it more than food, though. Unless you know where water is, never go into the wilderness without carrying some. Use a canteen to carry water. The canteen is made to hold water and keep it from spilling. It is strong and will not break easily.

In the desert, you can never be sure about water. The hotter the desert, the less chance you will find some. What you do find will often be filled with salt. Don't drink it.

Opposite: This water might be good to drink. But dangerous fish or plants that live in it might make the water off-limits to you.

If you are carrying something to drink when you get lost, you are very lucky. Drink as little of it as you can. Drink only a small amount every hour or so. When the weather is hot, drink a little more often. Drink as slowly as you can. Sip, don't gulp. You can never <u>be sure when you w</u>ill find good water.

Rain can be a good source of water. Watch for dark or growing clouds. Head toward them, and make sure you have something to catch the rain in. The top of a canteen makes a good rain catcher.

As you travel, look for large, solid, bowl-like objects. You will want to catch a lot of rain. You will also want to save a lot.

Water gathers in depressions on top of stones. Find a place where rock juts out of the ground. But watch out for snakes!

When you hear thunder and see lightning, don't try to collect rain. Move to safe shelter (see Chapter 7). Spread out clothing or large leaves in a double layer. They will give you a dry spot.

Stay away from the edges of rivers, lakes, or the ocean when it rains. There is always danger of a flood.

Moisture called *dew* collects on leaves of plants and trees. This happens in the early morning.

Opposite: The dew on tree and plant leaves is often a good source of water, but can make the ground damp and cold for sleeping. Jim collected dew to drink in the morning.

Carefully pour the dew into your container. You will be surprised how much water you can get!

Even mud can be a source of water. Squeeze the water out of it first. Then strain it over and over again until it is very clear. Use a piece of clothing as a strainer.

You can still gather water when there is no rain, even in the desert. Look for a damp or muddy spot in a dry riverbed or at the base of rocks and cliffs. Willows, cattails, greasewood, and other plants grow near underground water. Snow is the purest form of natural water. Ice, though, is hard to eat and can injure your mouth and throat. Try to melt it first. And taste a little of any snow or ice before you drink a lot. If it tastes salty or looks dirty, pass it up. You are better off thirsty than sick in the wilderness.

Thick plants and shrubs usually mean you can find water if you dig. But if the soil gets no wetter after about six inches (fifteen centimeters), dig somewhere else.

Rivers and lakes look like ideal sources of water — but they can be polluted. Follow the rule for snow and ice: Salty or dirty means pass it up. Look for signs of good water. When plants or trees grow close to the bank, it's a good bet. Swampy water is not good. Many different kinds of fish, and birds swooping around trying to catch them, usually mean the water is better.

The best idea with any water you find is to hope it is all right, but to figure that it isn't. Most of all, keep

Melting snow signals the end of winter. But it can also signal a sudden flood!

in mind that clean water can be made dirty if the container you drink it from is not clean. Wash your container really well before you drink out of it.

Mmm . . . doesn't that clean water taste good?

Chapter 4

A New Home

Finding some kind of shelter in the wilderness is not too hard.

Finding *safe* shelter is sometimes very hard.

Yet you need to get out of the wind, or rain, or sun, away from possible attack by animals or insects.

Someone might rescue you before dark. Then you will not need your shelter. But like Jim, you might have to stay in the wilderness through the night.

You should be ready.

Of course, if you have the time, you can build a shelter for yourself. But surviving in the wilderness is not the same as a planned camping trip. So it's better not to take the time to build something. Instead, use what the wilderness gives you.

Opposite: Many caves have natural stalactites — "icicles" made of limestone — hanging from their ceilings. They are beautiful, but they can break off and fall on you.

Look for shelter and get it ready for use before the sun goes down. If you have to sleep in the open, try to cover yourself with something. The air almost always becomes cooler than you expect at night. Even just some leaves on top of you can help you keep warm.

Even in what seems like endless snow, you can make a little home for yourself. Jim crawled in between two old logs. He could have broken off some tree branches and covered himself with them. Pine branches are best, if you can find some. The most important thing is to make sure you do not pick a place that can cave in on you. Never burrow in at the bottom of a hill of snow. Stay away from places where loose rocks can easily fall.

Speaking of "caving" in, a cave is sometimes a good place for shelter. But caves can sometimes cave in, too. Or they may have bats or other creatures that may be more of an enemy to you than what's outside. You can also get lost inside a cave.

If you find a cave-type shelter, take a good look at it from the outside. Walk around it. Feel the sides. Are they sturdy?

Once you are inside, take awhile to make sure that nothing can happen to block the entrance. Stay near the entrance, especially if you have no flashlight or matches. If you see anything suspicious,

Opposite: Pine trees thrive in cold areas. They stay green all year and their branches can be used for fire or shelter.

leave. An animal that is hurt, who could attack you, might have found the same cave.

Sleeping in the woods has its own problems — mainly insects and the chance of an unfriendly animal. Look for a spot that is well protected. Lightning often strikes trees, so do not go under one in a thunderstorm for any reason. Stay away from logs that might hold spiders, beehives, or animals that can bite. The best thing to do is to make a bed of leaves on smooth ground.

Though you might have seen people do it on television or in the movies, do not sleep up in a tree. You could fall out!

Don't sleep under a dead tree, either. You can tell a dead or dying tree because it has very few leaves. Sleeping under one on a windy night invites real trouble. They tend to fall over!

Do not sleep too near water. Ocean tides can come in while you are sleeping and soak you.

Moisture and tides, of course, are never a problem on the desert. Because there is so little water there, and so few trees, almost all deserts are very cold at night. But the desert itself provides ideal shelter from its heat and cold. Do what some desert animals do: Burrow into the sand with most of your body. Leave only your head free to breathe. In the daytime, help to shield yourself from the sun by keeping something above your head.

Opposite: Pools of water often form inside caves.

29

Chapter 5

Making a Fire – Escaping a Fire

If Jim had been lost longer in the wilderness, he might have wished he had a fire to help him survive. It is a good thing Jim was not lost too long—he did not know how to build a fire correctly!

You can use fire for everything from signaling for help and protecting yourself from animals to cooking food, sterilizing water, and keeping warm. But your fire must be under control. When fire is out of control, it can be the worst enemy of all.

No one should ever go into the wilderness without carrying a few matches. Be sure to wrap them in some material that keeps them dry no matter how wet you get. The best thing is to carry

Opposite: A forest fire is always a serious danger. Never stay in a "safe" place to watch a fire that is off in the distance. A sudden wind could blow the fire your way.

matches in two places, in case some of them get lost or wet.

Make sure lit matches are completely out before you throw them away. Touch the match head. Is it even a little bit warm? Hold the match in your hand until the head is completely cool.

There are many ways to make fire. Rubbing two dry sticks together, or striking steel against stone, makes sparks that make fire. But these are very difficult ways.

Eyeglasses, a flashlight lens, or even your watch crystal can make fire. Use the glass to concentrate the rays of the sun on a piece of paper or a dry leaf. The sun must be high in the sky, though.

No matter how you build a fire you must carefully choose the right site for it before you start. It should be a place that is sheltered, so a sudden rain or wind will not put out the fire. But do not build your fire where the flames can catch on something else—like low tree branches—and begin to spread. Never start a fire under any tree! A clifflike rock that juts out above you is good protection for a fire. You can also pile rocks as a fireplace, or dig a hole in windy weather.

Clear away a square area that is longer and wider than you are tall. Gather the driest wood you can find. Gather as much as you can before you light the

Opposite: Your protected patch of trees could go up in flames. Fire can quickly destroy a forest that took centuries to grow.

fire, because you should never leave a fire unwatched. Pile your extra wood far away from where you are building the fire.

Water, if you have enough, is the best way to put out a fire. When you have no water, do it this way: Let your fire die down as far as you can. Scatter the coals. Dig some dirt from nearby and pour it over the fire. Dig a small hole and sweep the fire's remains into it. Cover the hole with dirt.

Be sure you get all of it. Place your hand on the "fire" and leave it there one minute. Do not leave until the fire site is *completely* cool. Just one hot coal can smolder into a huge forest fire! The tidal wave of flames can engulf a huge area and everything in it—including you!

Always build a fire with your back to the wind, as Jim did. That way you will not get smoke in your face and loose coals will not blow onto your clothing.

Here are two ways to make a fire.

Easy way.

1. Gather two handfuls of the driest grasses, leaves, paper, or tiny twigs. (This is called *tinder*.)

2. Break up some sticks of different sizes.

3. Light the tinder.

4. Stuff the tinder under a small stack of twigs.

5. As each layer of twigs catches fire, add larger and larger twigs.

Hard way.

1. On your fire site, make an A with sticks. Keep the open end of the A toward the wind.

2. On top of the A's crossbar, place a small pile of tinder.

3. Face the fire with your back to the wind.

4. Strike the match toward the wood. Reach under the tinder with the burning match to start the fire.

5. As the fire begins to burn, stand bigger pieces of wood *(kindling)* over it. Place them in a tepee or pyramid design.

6. If you have to, burn some of your clothing. Don't burn too much of it. You might need it for warmth later.

7. Unless you are using your fire as a signal, always keep it small.

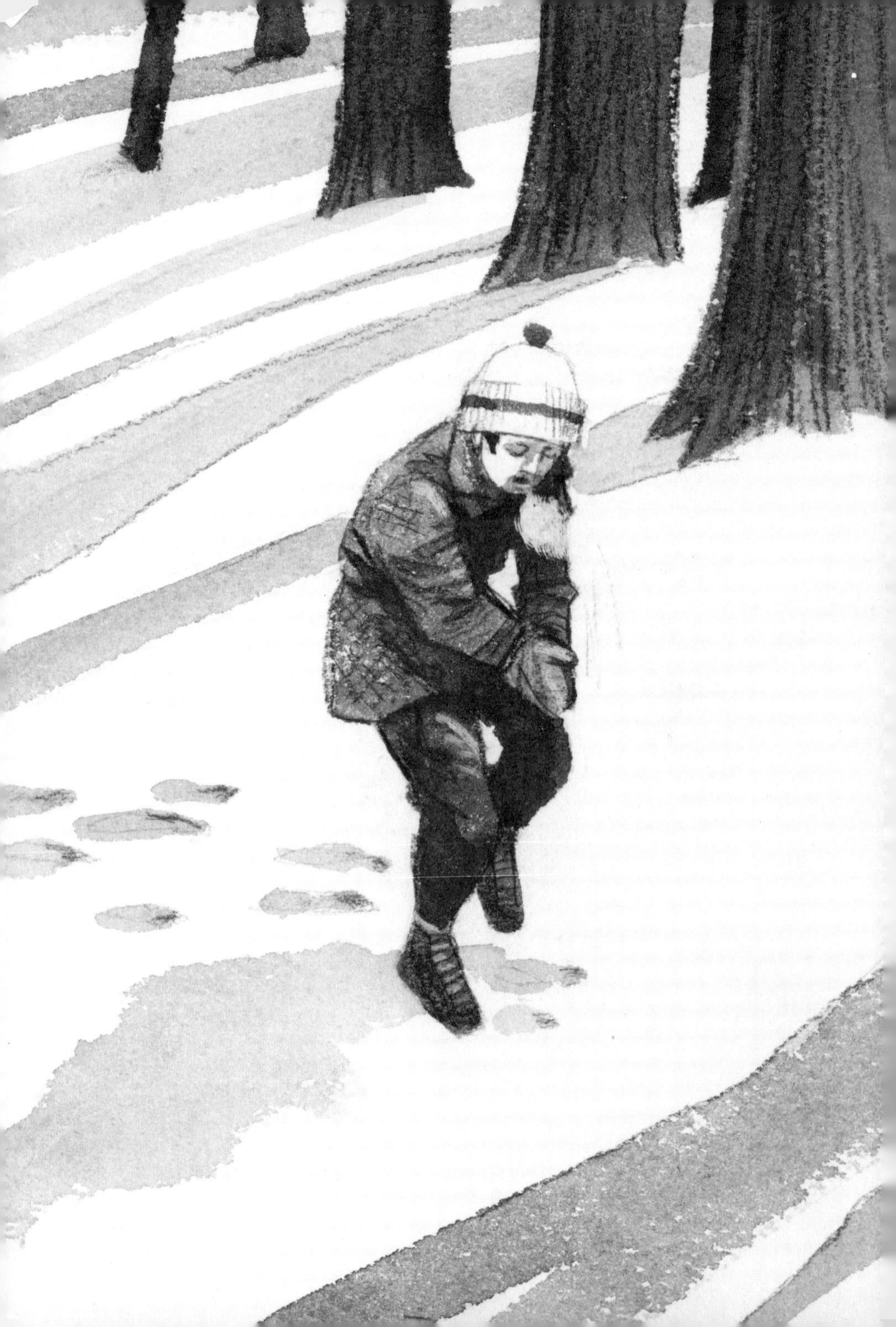

Chapter 6

Beating Heat and Cold

They are invisible.

Yet though you cannot see them, heat and cold can hurt you more than an attacking animal or a fantastic flood. And because you cannot see them, heat and cold can sneak up on you, slowly but surely breaking you down. To beat them, the first thing is to *know* that it is *getting too cold*—or *too hot.*

What do you do at the first sign?

If you have been sweating for an hour or more, and the air seems to be getting warmer, take action then and there. First, move out of the sunlight's path, if you can. Find a spot where there is shade, or make your own shade. Stand some sticks in the

Opposite: Moving around in cold weather is one way to keep warm. But don't work up a sweat or you will be chilled even more.

ground and spread a garment over them to make a tent. Stay under there until clouds come and cool the air, or until late in the afternoon when the sun loses its power.

Heat can make you very tired. It is better to save your power and move toward safety when coolness comes.

Cool air is heavier than warm air, so look for the lowest part of the land. Even water that might be too dirty to drink can cool your body. Do not jump into it. Just splash it lightly all over yourself. Later, when your body is less warm, slowly enter the water to rest for a few minutes. Do not fall asleep! Do not go away from the shore or swim if you are alone. It will take awhile for your clothes to dry, which will give you added time to stay cool.

Wind can also cool you. But if the wind is calm, fan yourself with a piece of clothing or a leafy branch from a bush.

Cold can be even more of an enemy than heat. When you are too hot, you can rest. But when you are too cold, you must keep moving or your body will freeze.

Movement is the first and best way to keep your body warm. And do not move only your legs, by walking. Jump up and down. Clap your hands. Make faces. It's better to be a little tired than too cold.

Even if you have gloves on, keep your hands inside your shirt or coat. Leave your shoes or boots on. Severe frostbite can permanently damage fingers, toes, and other body parts—like your nose. Lift your collar or scarf, pull down your headgear—do whatever you can. But do not leave your head completely bare. A vast amount of body heat can escape through your scalp, and you will feel even colder.

If your hands, feet, or face become frostbitten do not rub them with snow. That makes it worse! Touch the frostbitten parts of your body gently to another, warmer body part. Cup a warm hand over a cold ear. Put a frostbitten hand in an armpit.

Your biggest enemies in the cold are wind and rain. Most people think that if it rains, it is not so cold. But when the temperature is near freezing, rain can make you even colder, just as water cools you off when you are warm. If dry leaves are plentiful, pile them thickly before the rain comes. When the rain stops, push the top layers of leaves away and roll on the dry leaves until you are dry, too.

Wind, like rain, can make you colder. Protect yourself from it by hiding behind a natural barrier—a tree, rock, or hill.

Finally, protect yourself against the biggest enemy of all—fear. You can run away from a fire or an attacking animal, but you cannot run away from the heat and cold. But if you keep your "cool," you can beat them.

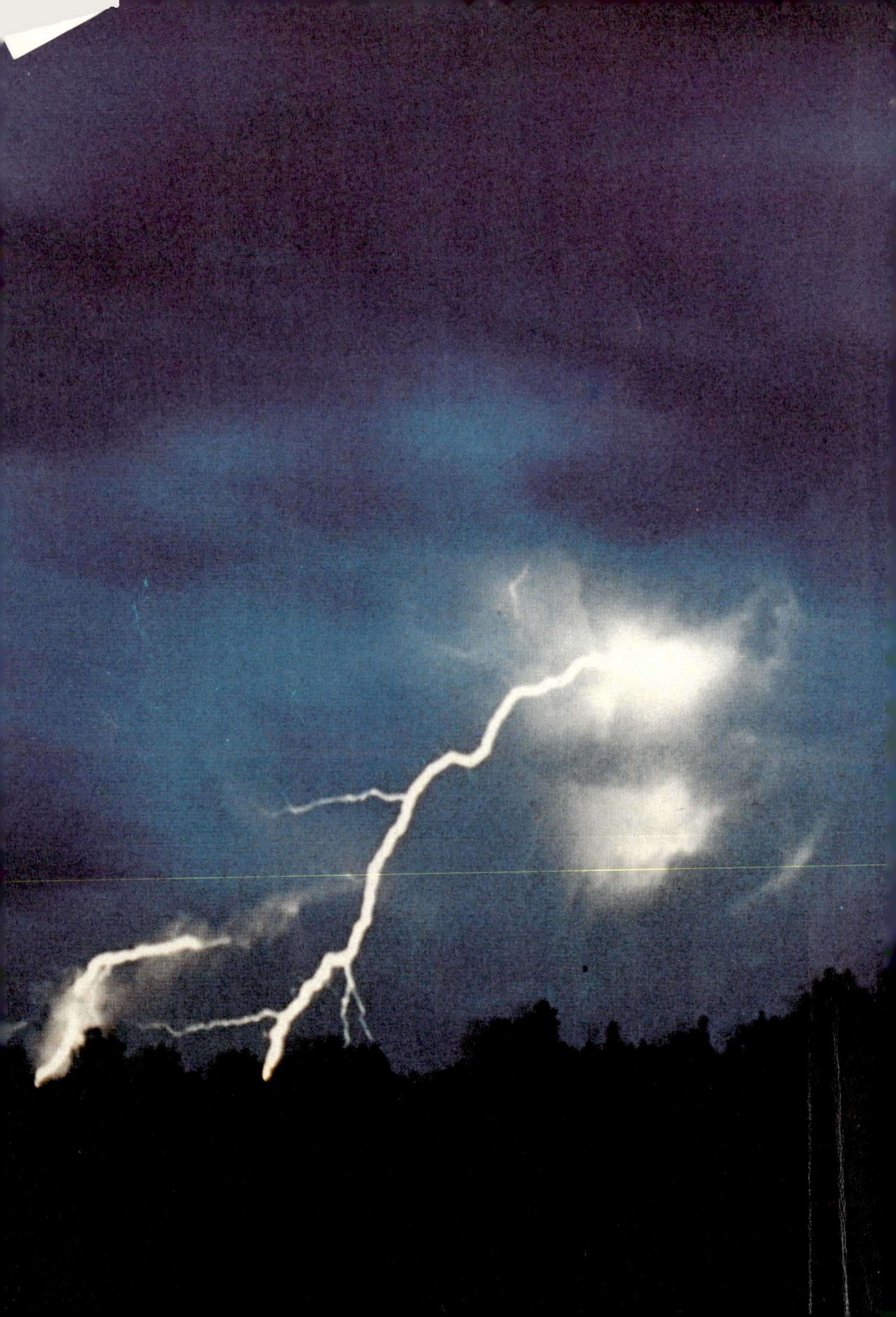

Chapter 7

Beating the Weather

Nothing is as powerful in this world as the winds and water of the wilderness—when you are not prepared for them.

No one can stand in the path of a cyclone or hurricane. Even a thunderstorm with high winds can cause terrible damage. What you must do is watch for the signs that something extreme might be happening in the weather, and make sure you are in a safe place *before* it happens.

Tidal waves and hurricanes, of course, happen only on the seacoast near oceans. Scientists know when there is danger of these great walls of waves and wind.

Opposite: Lightning is nature's fireworks, but it is nothing to celebrate. It is many times more powerful than dynamite and can do much more damage.

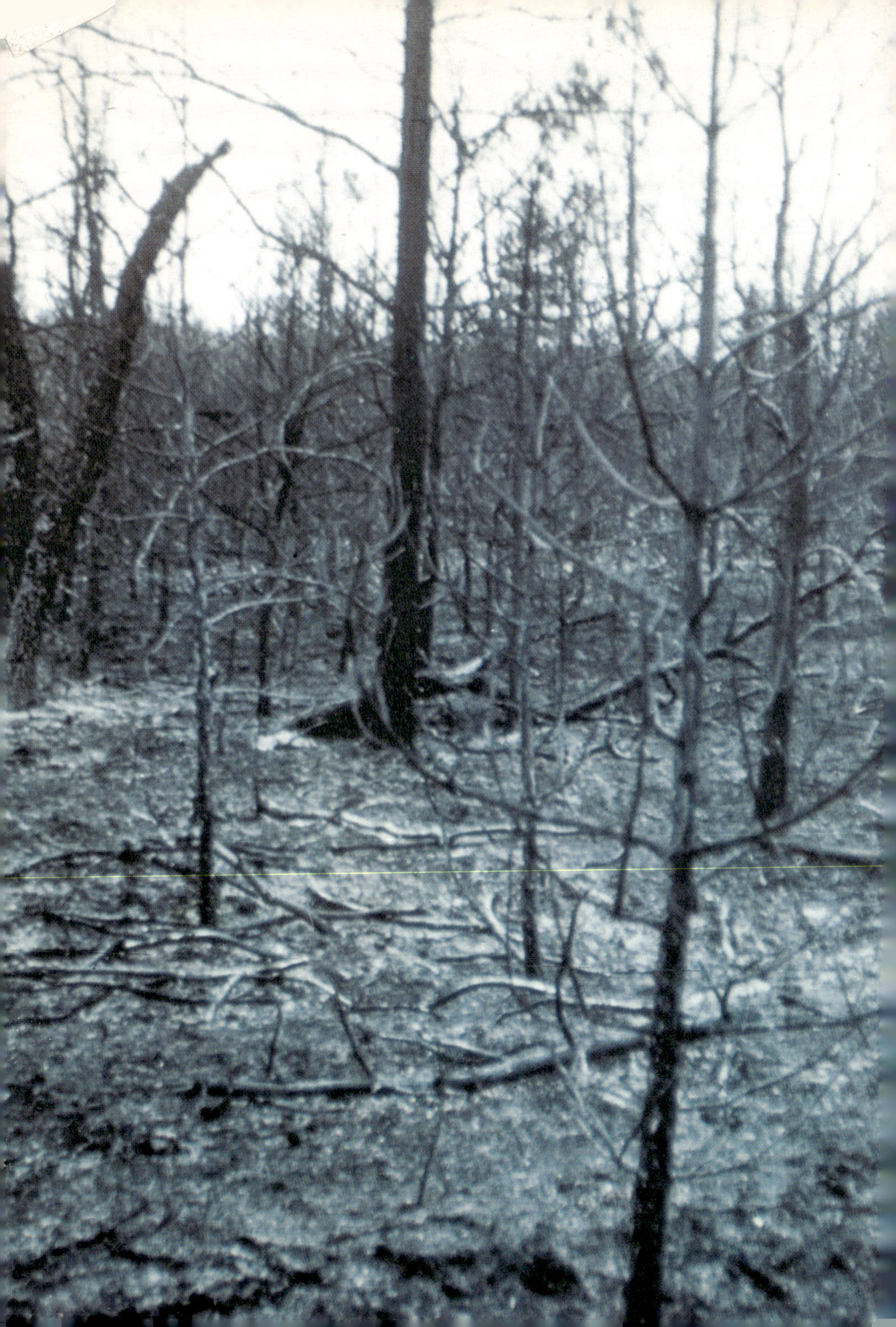

Thunderstorms are a common severe form of weather. Dark, large clouds, moving fast, usually mean thunderstorms are coming. Look for shelter right away, but do not go too high up. The higher something reaches into the sky, the more chance that lightning can hit it. The paths of cyclones and tornados are more difficult to predict. These paths are usually about one-quarter-mile (one-half-kilometer) wide. Move toward one side of the path as fast as you can.

If you see a thunderstorm approaching, or the wind changes suddenly, lie flat in a ravine or any other low spot—but not where anything can fall on you—until the storm leaves the area. Never hide under a tree! Not only can it fall when blown down, but lightning can strike it—and you.

In mountain country a great wall of snow can form and slide down the mountain in an *avalanche*. Do not walk over snow shelves or at the bottoms of steep slopes, especially after a new snowfall. If you see an avalanche coming, roll your body into a ball. It will be easier to move and dig your way out.

Remember: It is important to watch what is moving toward you. Watching where you are moving is not enough.

Opposite: The hardest thing for a forest to survive is a fire—but it does! The ashes from these fallen giants will create fertile ground for new trees to grow in.

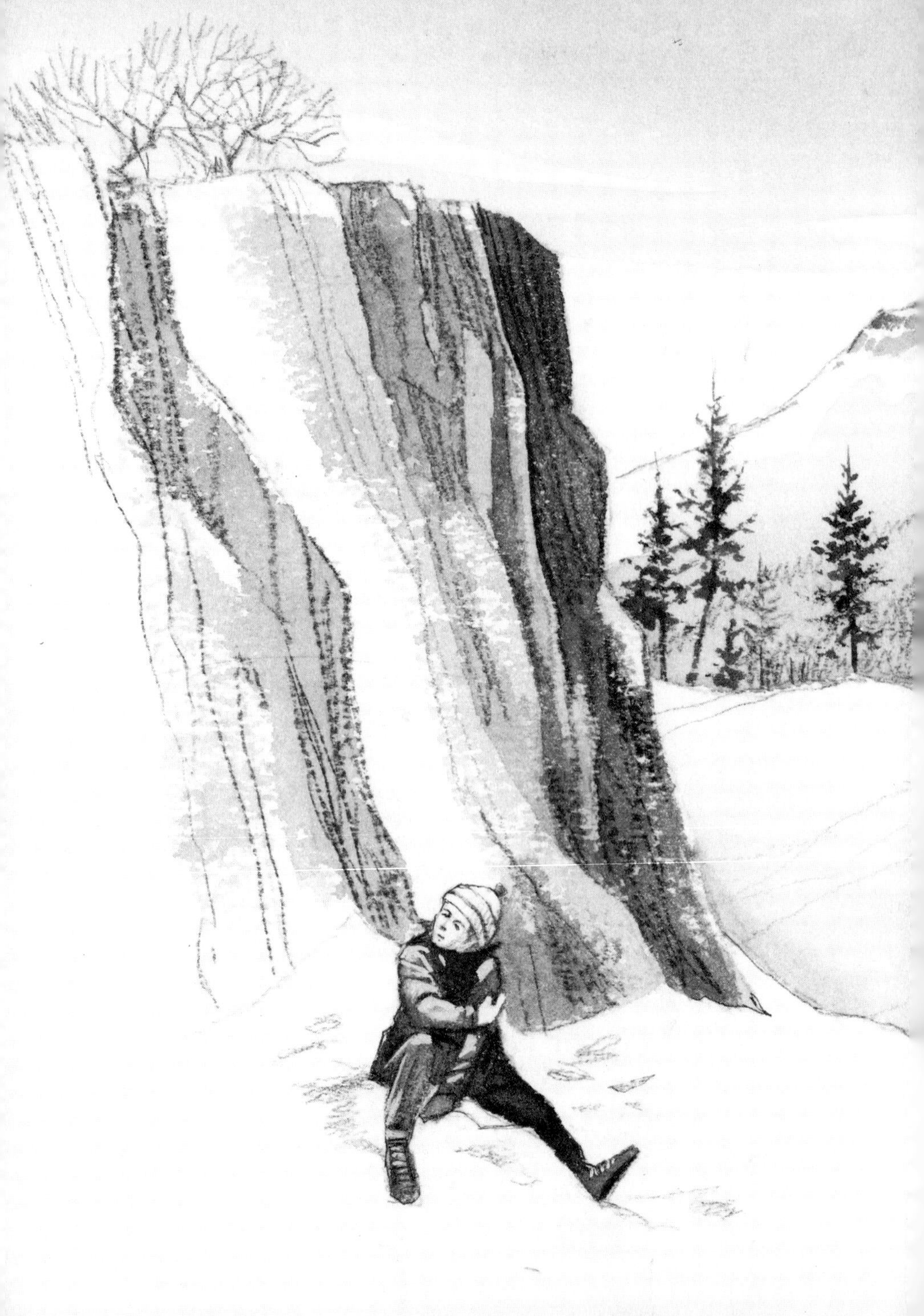

Chapter 8

Avoiding Accidents

Jim would never play basketball with one hand tied behind his back. Would you?

Well, it's even worse when you are lost in the wilderness to have "one hand tied behind your back." And that's what can happen if you are injured.

Most accidents happen because we did not watch where we were going, or because we took a risk that was not necessary. When Jim was lost, for instance, he saw a high cliff. He thought, "If I can only get up there, I might be able to see for miles around. Then I would know which way to go."

Opposite: Avoid climbing cliffs, especially in winter. Ice or rocks made brittle by the cold could make you lose your footing.

He began to climb. But the rock was covered with ice and slippery. About halfway up, after he almost fell twice, he decided to stop. He realized that it was silly to take more risk. First, maybe he would not be able to see enough from there. Second, what if he could not get down without falling?

As a matter of fact, Jim did fall. But he fell only about ten feet to the ground. Luckily, he merely bruised his arm. If he had broken it — or his leg — he might never have been able to find shelter for the night. He might not have survived until morning!

What do you do if you injure yourself?

If you sprain or fracture a bone, it will probably swell up. Keep the injured part of your body as still as possible. That way there will be less pain and less chance of further injury.

When you cut yourself, clean the wound as well as you can. See Chapter 10 to learn how.

If you are dizzy, or bleeding — or most important, if you have fainted even for a short time — lie down for a while. Get up slowly. If you are still dizzy, lie down again. Wait until there are no more signs, except possibly pain, of something serious.

Before you ever go near the wilderness you should know something about first aid. You can study it in school, in clubs and organizations, at camp, and many other places. Your teacher will be able to tell you where to find first aid classes. Knowing first aid will give you the good feeling of

A rabbit's fur blends with the snow to keep the animal from being seen and injured by other creatures. We must rely on our good sense to stay safe in the wilderness.

helping yourself or someone else when an injury occurs. The time and study first aid courses require will seem less important then.

Chances are you will not have an accident in the wilderness. But keep in mind that it is better to prevent an accident than to care for yourself when you have one.

Watch where you walk.

Be careful where you climb.

Be sure that a doctor checks any injury as soon as you get out of the wilderness.

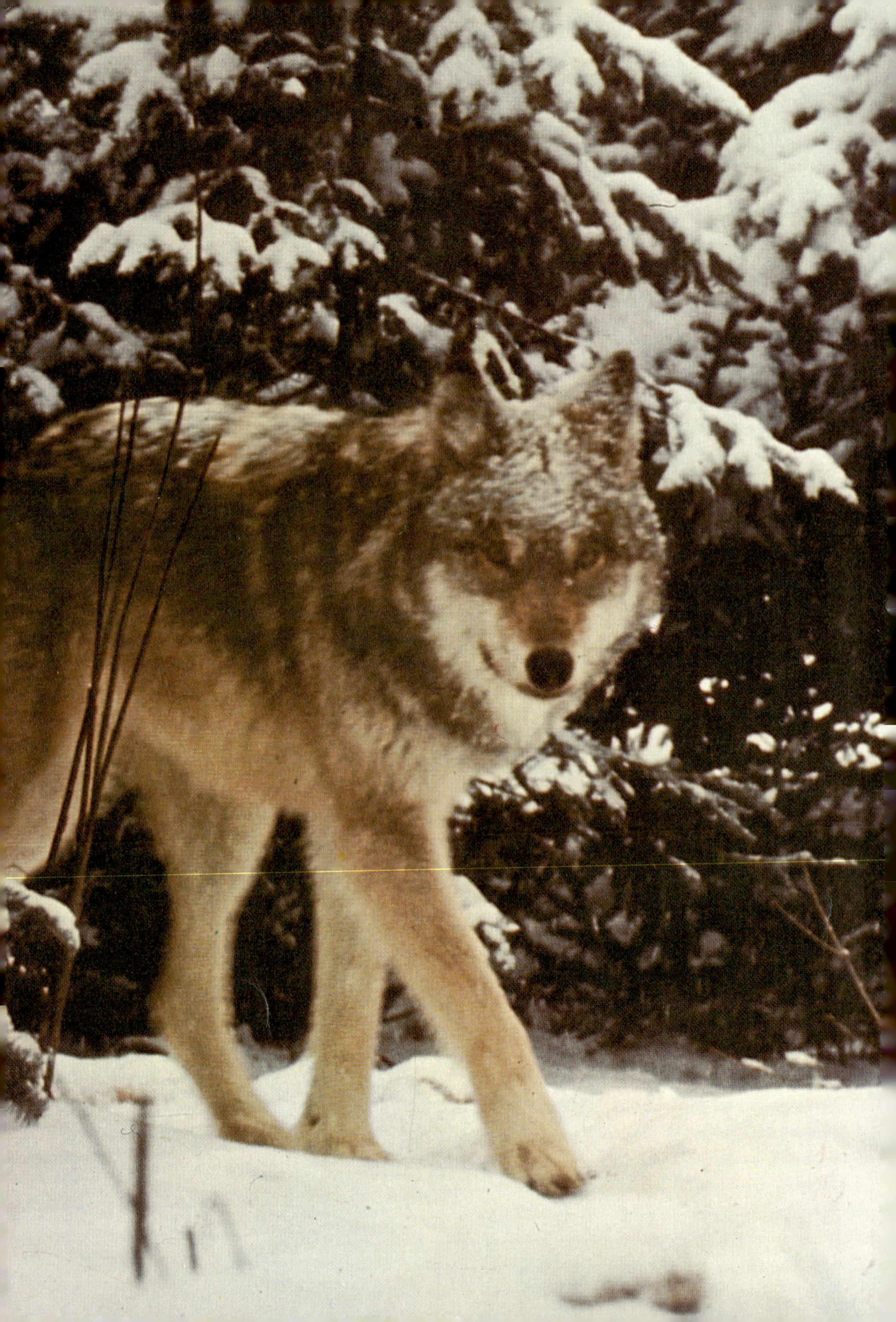

Chapter 9

Attack!

There are many different creatures in the wilderness. You can protect yourself best by knowing the rules that apply to almost all wild animals.

The first rule to know is this: You usually do not have to worry about an animal attacking you. Not every living creature is friendly, but they do like to keep to themselves. Hardly ever will they bother you if you do not bother them.

There is one time when that is not true: when an animal is sick or hurt. A wild animal that does not scamper away, or a bird that does not fly away, might be in trouble. When it sees anything unusual, it might feel that more trouble is coming, and attack. So the animals you can get closest to in nature are

Opposite: Wolves normally travel in groups and are shy. If a bold, lone wolf heads your way, watch out! It might be ill and it could injure you. Pages 50-51: Animals carefully watch other creatures who move near them. They move out of the way, and so should you!

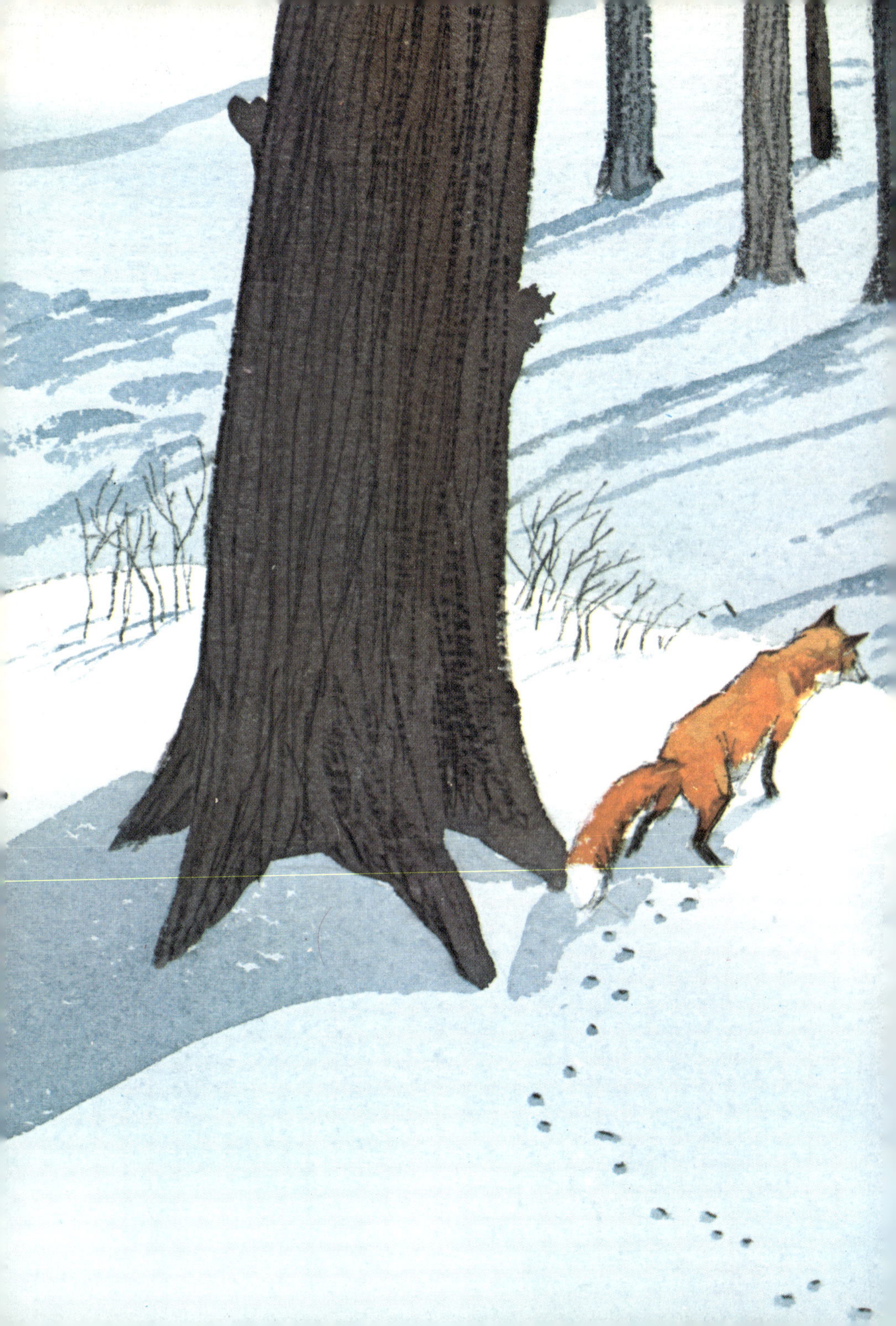

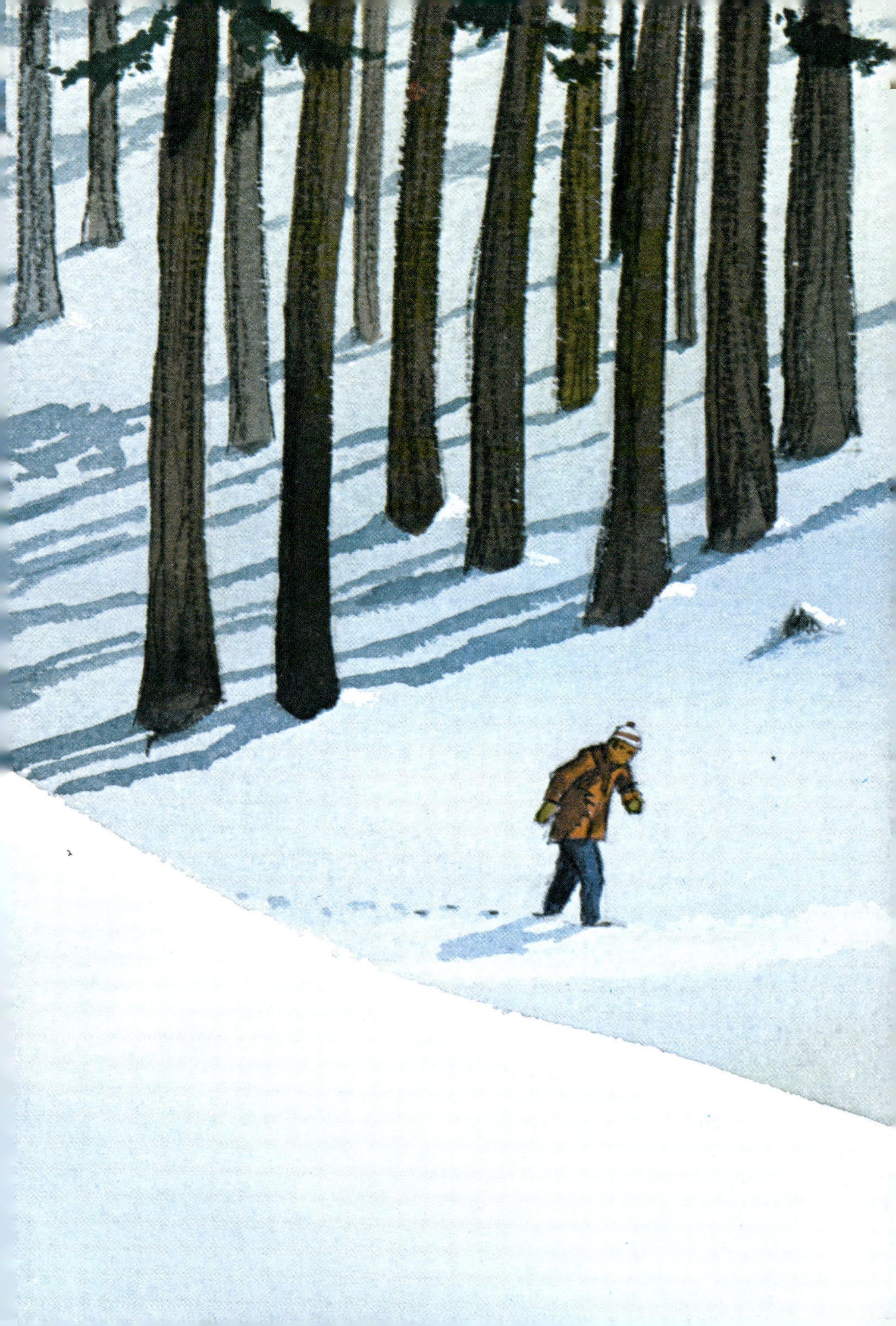

the ones you must watch out for whenever you are in the wilderness.

Most hurt or sick animals will hide. They want to protect themselves from other animals and give themselves time to recover. This is why you should use the clearest path possible. Thick, tall underbrush always holds some risk. Old logs do, too. You can safely sit on one at the beach, but stay away from them in the wilds. Jim was very lucky that nothing was hiding in the logs he found. Caves and marshy ground are often hiding places, too.

A mother trying to protect her young might also attack you if you get too close. Do not try to look at the babies, even though they are cute.

Animals rest in hidden places, too. If you step near them there, they might naturally react by biting or stinging you.

Observe animals in nature from a distance. They are not meant to be seen close up—and never are naturally tame. Once again: *The wild animal that will let you get too close is the most dangerous of all.*

Creatures who do not move around much, such as snakes, are a special threat. While a bird can fly away quickly, and a fox can scamper speedily to safety, a snake might lie still as you pass. And when you pass too close, it might bite you!

Probably the worst danger of attack in the wilderness is from the smallest creatures of all—

Snakes are hard to see in thick brush even when you are very careful. When you go into the wilderness, wear thick-soled shoes that snakes cannot bite through.

insects. They are so small that it is hard to see them. Spiders, for instance, tend to blend in with the background. They can be under a single leaf or a piece of bark on a tree. Second, insects are almost everywhere. In a way you are always invading their territory.

Bees and wasps are even more of a threat than spiders. They might sting you, even if you have not bothered them. On humid and warm days, it is hard to avoid mosquitoes in the wilderness. These tiny insects can land lightly on you and bite you before you know it. Their bite in itself does not mean much. But mosquitoes often carry diseases that they can transmit to you. Stay away from low, wet, overgrown areas. The most mosquitoes—and many hidden dangers—lie there!

Chapter 10

Avoiding Infection

Did you do all these things and were still bitten or clawed by an animal? Here is what to do:

Clean the wound immediately. Start by rubbing around it gently with a piece of your clothing. *Do not touch the wound with your fingers.* More trouble comes from infection than from the wound itself!

Squeeze deep wounds before you clean them. Blood should come out, but so will germs. Pull out the stinger of a bee or wasp.

Then sterilize the tip of a knife or other sharp metal object to clean the wound itself. Hold the tip in the flame of two or three matches lit one after the other. The knife tip will get anything out of the wound that does not belong there. Gently scrape away blood or dirt from right outside the wound. Be very gentle—and remember, this might hurt.

Most forest animals such as this wolverine have sharp claws and teeth. They use these to find and eat their food.

Always clean *away* from a wound, not into it.

Wash the wound with the cleanest water you can find. Cover the wound with a torn-off piece of your clothing or something similar. Make the dressing firm enough so it does not come off and dirt does not get in.

Remember: No animal carries a grudge against you. Most animals do not want to attack a person. They only want you to watch where you walk — because the wilderness is their home.

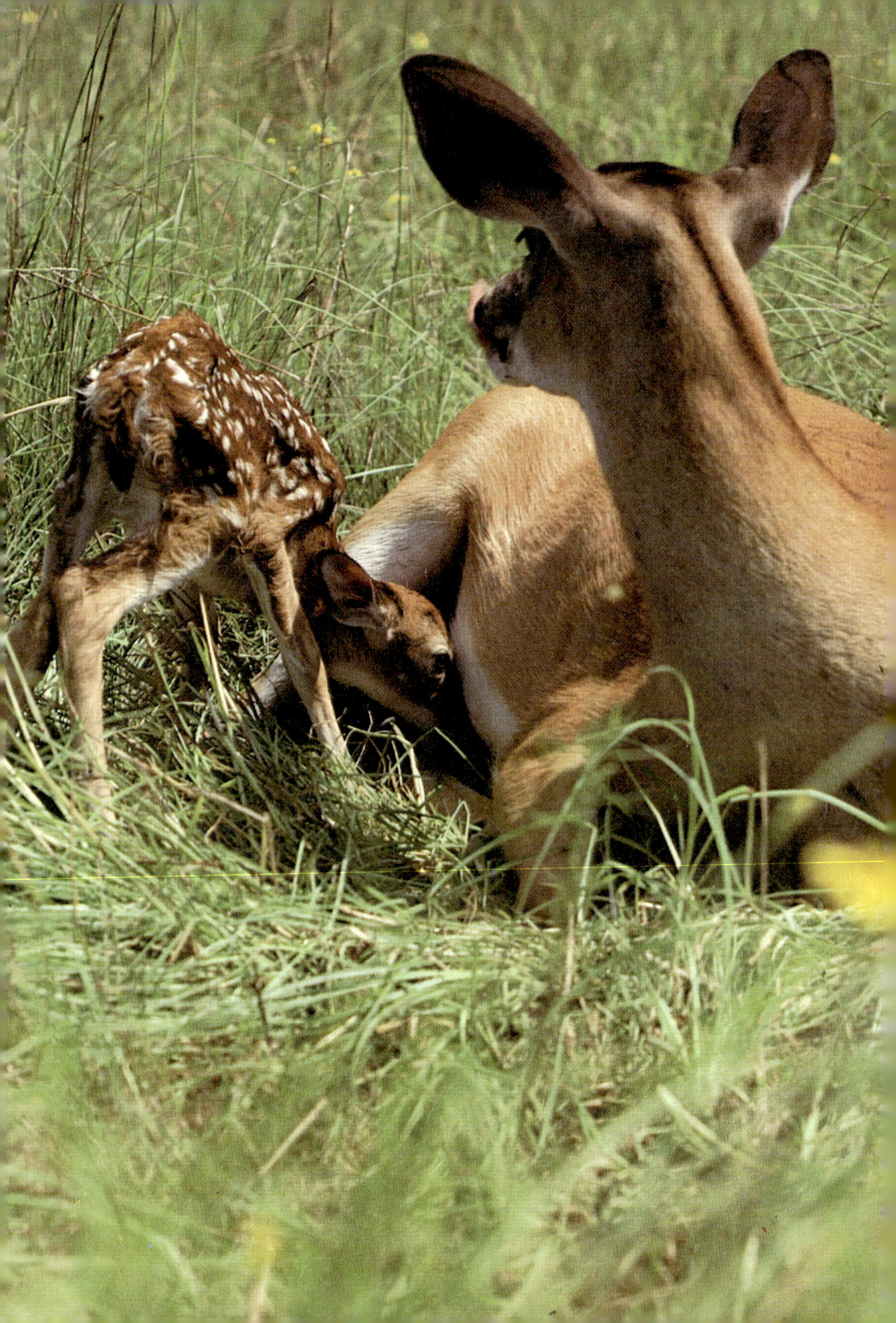

Chapter 11

The Wilderness Is Yours

Now it is up to you to "write" your own story on surviving in the wilderness. How? By going out into nature.

Nature is usually your friend. But nature can also be a danger. You must know what to do when it becomes your enemy. Then it will be your friend again.

In this book, you saw the most important times and places that nature can work against you. You learned what to do when things go wrong in the wilderness. Now you can truly enjoy the trees and the sky, the snow and the sun, the rain and the wind—and the animals that live in the outdoors.

Opposite: The wilderness is home to many beautiful animals like this deer and her fawn. They have learned to survive everything but careless people.

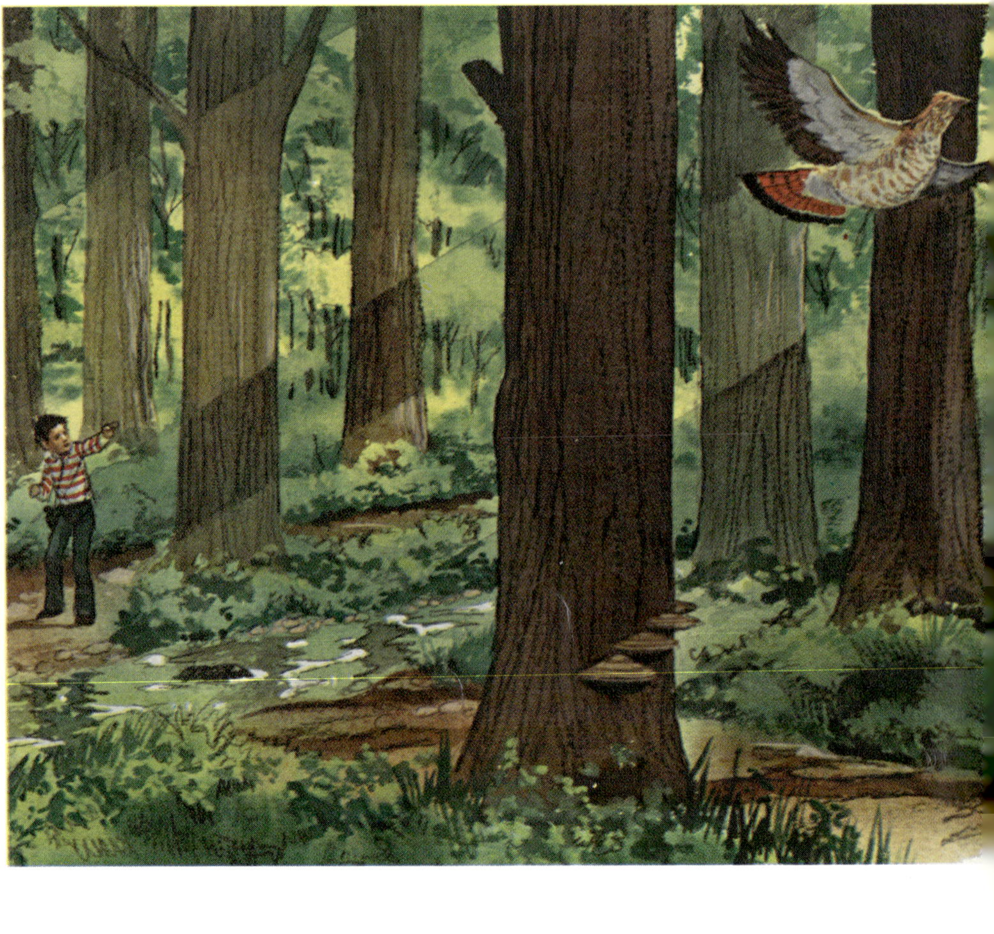

Inside every one of us, under the daily cares that surround our lives, is the need—and the desire—to go back to nature now and then.

When we make fine grades in school, when we achieve excellence in some sport, when we make a new friend, we feel good about ourselves in a certain way. Each of us needs a special victory all our own. The victory of surviving in nature gives us that feeling.

Close your eyes for a moment.

Can you feel the warm sun pouring down on you as you enter a forest that has been growing for maybe hundreds of years? Can you hear the water of a fresh, rippling stream? Do you see a bird, or maybe a beaver, or some creature that you have never, ever seen before?

Open your eyes. What would it be like if you were really standing in that forest, or near that stream, or on that mountainside? Wouldn't you be happy?

Opposite: When you are surrounded by trees and wildlife, you are a part of the wilderness.

For further reading

Accerrano, Anthony J., **The Outdoorman's Emergency Manual,** New York: Winchester Press, 1976.

Blanchard, Marjorie P., **The Outdoor Cookbook,** New York: F. Watts, 1977.

Bridge, Raymond, **High Peaks and Clear Roads: A Safe and Easy Guide to Outdoor Skills,** Englewood Cliffs, N.J.: Prentice-Hall, 1978.

Brown, Vinson, **Knowing the Outdoors in the Dark,** Harrisburg, Pa.: Stackpole Books, 1973.

Dalrymple, Byron W., **Survival in the Outdoors,** New York: Outdoor Life, 1972.

Merrill, Wilfred Kerner, **The Survival Handbook,** New York: Arco, 1974.

Olsen, Larry Dear, **Outdoor Survival Skills,** New York: Pocket Books, 1976.

Sattler, Helen Roney, **Nature's Weather Forecasters,** 1st ed., Nashville: T. Nelson, 1978.

Vandenburg, Mary Lou, **Help!: Emergencies That Could Happen to You and How to Handle Them,** Minneapolis: Lerner Publications Co., 1975.

Index

A (fire), 35
Accidents (also see Injury), 45, 47, 62
Afternoon, 37
Air, 37, 38
Alone, 7, 10, 13, 38, 61
Animals, 13, 17, 25, 26, 29, 31, 37, 39, 47, 49, 50-51, 52, 54, 55, 56, 57, 62
Arm, 46
Armpit, 39
Attack, 25, 37, 39, 49, 52, 55
Attention, Attracting, 16
Avalanche, 43

Bats, 26
Beaver, 58
Beehives, 29
Bees, 29, 53, 54
Birds, 23, 49, 52, 59
Bites, 52, 53, 54
Bleeding, 46
Blood, 54
Body, 38, 39, 43, 46
Boots, 38
Branches, Tree, 16, 26, 32, 38
Bravery, 10
Breathing, 29
Bruise, 46
Building, 25
Burrowing, 26

Can, Metal, 16
Canteen, 19, 20, 61
Cattails, 22
Caves, 24, 25, 26, 28, 29, 52
Clapping, 38
Cleaning, 46, 54, 62
Cliffs, 22, 32, 44, 45
Climbing, 45, 46, 47, 62
Clothing, 16, 20, 22, 34, 35, 38, 54
Cloth, White, 16, 61
Clouds, 20, 38, 43
Coals, 34
Coat, 38
Cold (also see Coolness), 11, 29, 37, 39, 45, 62

Collar, 39
Color, 16
Colorado, 7
Container, Water, 19, 20, 23
Cooking, 31, 62
Coolness (also see Cold), 32, 38
Creatures (also see Animals), 47, 49, 52, 59
Cyclone, 11, 41, 43

Danger (also see Enemies), 19, 52, 57, 62
Dark, 10, 24
Day, 16, 29
Deer, 56, 57
Desert, 16, 19, 22, 29
Dew, 20, 21, 22
Digging, 22, 32, 34, 43
Dirt, 34, 54, 55
Disease (also see Illness), 53
Dizziness, 46
Doctor, 47, 62
Dressing, 55
Dry, Staying, 20, 31, 39, 62

Equipment (also see Clothing, Matches, Flashlight), 12, 61
Ear, 39
Enemies (also see Danger), 13, 26, 31, 38, 56
Energy, 17, 38, 61
Eyeglasses, 32

Face, 39
Fainting, 46
Falling, 46
Fan, 38
Fear, 10, 13, 39, 61
Feet, 39
Fingers, 39, 54
Fire (also see Flame), 16, 26, 30-35, 39, 43, 62
First aid, 46, 47
Fish, 19, 22
Flame (also see Fire), 54
Flashlight, 16, 26, 32, 61
Flood, 20

61

Food, 19, 62
Forest (also see Woods), 32, 42, 43, 58
Forest fire, 30, 31, 32, 33, 34
Fox, 52
Freezing, 38, 39
Frostbite, 39

Garment(s) (also see Clothing), 38
Glass, 32
Gloves, 38
Grass, 35
Greasewood, 22
Ground, 16, 20, 29, 38

Hands, 38, 39
Head, 29, 39
Headgear, 39
Heat (also see Hot), 11, 29, 37, 38, 39
Hiding, 13, 43, 52
High, 16, 43, 44
Home, 25, 26, 55
Hot (also see Heat), 18, 19, 20, 62
Humidity, 53
Hurricane, 40

Ice, 22, 45
Illness (also see Disease), 22, 48, 49, 52
Infection, 54, 62
Injury (also see Accidents), 22, 45, 46, 47, 62
Insects, 25, 29, 53

Jumping, 38

Kindling, 35
Knife, 54

Lakes, 20, 22, 29
Leaves, 20, 26, 29, 32, 35, 39, 53
Legs, 38, 46
Light, 16
Lightning, 20, 29, 40, 41, 43
Logs, 16, 26, 29, 52
Lost, Being, 7, 10, 11, 17, 26, 31, 45, 61

Marks, Trail, 7, 10
Marsh (also see Swamp), 52
Matches, 62
Metal, 16, 54
Mirror, 16

Moisture, 16, 29
Morning, 20, 46
Mosquitoes, 53
Mountain, 6, 7, 10, 43, 59
Movement, 37, 38, 52
Mud, 22

Nature, 49, 52, 57, 59, 62
Night, 10, 16, 25, 46
Noise, 17
Nose, 39

Ocean, 20, 29, 41
Organizations, 46
Outdoors (also see Nature, Wilderness), 57

Paper, 32, 35
Path, 43, 52
Plants, 20, 22
Pollution, 22
Protection, 10, 19, 31, 32, 49, 52, 62
Pyramid, 35

Rain, 20, 25, 32, 39, 57
Ravine, 43
Reflection, 16
Rescue, 11, 17, 25, 61
Risk, 45, 46, 52
Riverbed, Dry, 22
Rivers, 20, 22, 29
Rock(s), 20, 22, 26, 32, 39, 45
Rules, 61
Running, 7

Safety, 16, 19, 20, 25, 41, 52, 61, 62
Salt, 19, 22
Sand, 16, 29
Scalp, 39
Scarf, 39
School, 46
Scientists, 41
Seacoast (also see Ocean), 41
Senses, Five, 17
Shelter, 13, 14-15, 20, 25, 26, 28, 32, 43, 46, 61
Shirt, 38
Shoes, 38, 53
Shrubs, 16, 22
Signals, 16, 17, 30, 35, 61, 62
Signs, 41, 46
Sky, 16, 32, 57

Sleep, 20, 21, 26, 28, 38, 62
Smoke signals, 16
Snakes, 20, 52, 53
Snow, 6, 7, 10, 12, 13, 16, 22, 23, 26, 39, 43, 47, 57
Soil (also see Dirt), 22
S.O.S., 12, 13, 16
Sparks, 32
Spiders, 29, 53
Splashing, 38
Stalactite, 24, 25
Sterilizing, 31, 54, 62
Sting, 52, 53, 54
Sticks (also see Twigs), 37
Stones (also see Rocks), 16, 20
Stream (also see River, Water), 58
Straining, 22
Strength, 18
Strip, Luminous, 17
Sun, 11, 16, 24, 26, 29, 32, 37, 56, 58, 62
Survival, 11, 13, 25, 46, 57, 59, 61
Swamp, 22
Sweating, 37
Swimming, 38

Teacher, 46
Temperature, 39
Tepee, 35
Thunder, 20
Thunderstorm, 29, 41, 43
Tidal wave, 41
Tide, 29
Tinder, 35

Toes, 39
Tornado (also see Cyclone), 43
Tracks, 7, 8-9
Trail, 7
Tree(s), 7, 10, 20, 22, 26, 27, 29, 32, 39, 43, 53, 57, 58, 59
Twigs (also see Branches), 16, 35

Underbrush (also see Grass), 52
Underground, 22

Walking, 7, 26, 38, 47, 55, 62
Warmth, 26, 31, 36, 37, 38, 39, 53, 62
Wasp, 53, 54
Watch crystal, 32
Water, 17, 18-23, 28, 29, 31, 34, 38, 41, 55, 59, 61, 62
Wave, Tidal, 41
Weather, 20, 32, 36, 37, 41, 62
Whistle, 16, 61
Wilderness (also see Wilds), 19, 22, 25, 31, 41, 45, 46, 47, 49, 52, 53, 55, 57, 59, 61, 62
Wilds (also see Wilderness), 52
Willows, 22
Wind, 10, 25, 29, 31, 32, 34, 38, 39, 41, 43, 57
Wolf, 48, 49
Wolverine, 55
Wood, Fire, 32, 34, 35
Woods (also see Forest), 16, 29
Wounds, 46, 54, 55, 62